From the desktop of Jeffrey Simmons

A vacation in Paris inspired Miroslav Sasek to create childrens travel guides to the big cities of the world. He brought me *This is Paris* in 1958 when I was publishing in London, and we soon followed up with *This is London*. Both books were enormously successful, and his simple vision grew to include more than a dozen books. Their amusing verse, coupled with bright and charming illustrations, made for a series unlike any other, and garnered Sasek (as we always called him) the international and popular acclaim he deserved.

I was thrilled to learn that *This is Hong Kong* will once again find its rightful place on bookshelves. Sasek is no longer with us (and I have lost all contact with his family), but I am sure he would be delighted to know that a whole new generation of wide-eyed readers is being introduced to his whimsical, imaginative, and enchanting world.

Your name here

Published by arrangement with Simon & Schuster Books for Young Readers,
Simon & Schuster Children's Publishing Division

This edition first published in the United States of America in 2007 by
UNIVERSE PUBLISHING
A Division of Rizzoli International Publications, Inc.
300 Park Avenue South
New York, NY 10010
www.rizzoliusa.com

© Miroslav Sasek, 1965

*See updated Hong Kong facts at end of book

2012 2013 2014 2015 / 10 9 8 7 6

Printed in China

ISBN–10: 0-7893-1560-2
ISBN–13: 978-0-7893-1560-1

Library of Congress Control Number: 2006907091

Cover design: centerpointdesign

M. Sasek

THIS IS HONG KONG

UNIVERSE

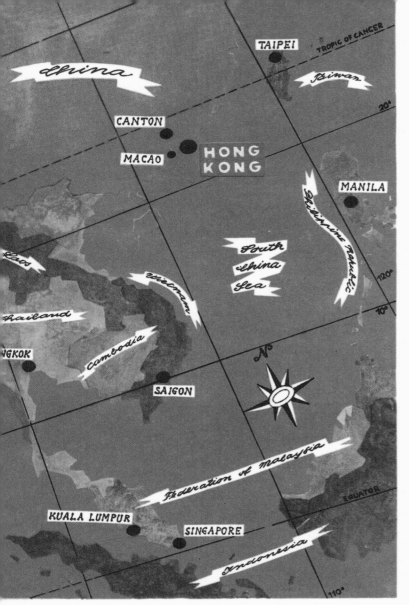

Hong Kong lies on the south coast of continental China, 70 nautical miles below the Tropic of Cancer on the South China Sea. It has a land surface of 425 square miles and was a British Crown Colony for almost 150 years. Kowloon and the New Territories, by far the largest part of the total area, are on the mainland; the rest consists of 236 mostly uninhabited islands. Hong Kong Island — 50 square miles — with its city of Victoria, the capital, is the heart of the region. It lies opposite Kowloon. Both were ceded by China to the British Crown in perpetuity. The New Territories, bordering on China, and Lantau, the largest island, were leased to Great Britain in 1898. The lease expired in 1997.*

To transform the map of Hong Kong into breathtakingly beautiful reality, you take an eight-minute cable-car ride on the Peak Tram.

Below you (see overleaf), Victoria City; across Victoria Harbour, Kowloon peninsula backed by a mountain ridge. Behind the ridge, the New Territories stretch some twenty miles to the Chinese border.

Thousands of passengers and vehicles are carried daily by ferries between Kowloon and Victoria. The Star Ferries alone transport 74,000 people a day.

You get this priceless view, plus the ferry ride across the Harbour, for $2.20 (Hong Kong) or thirty cents (U.S.).

220,000 vessels of all kinds call at Victoria Harbour every year.

The Harbour used to be visited by opium traders, pirates, and typhoons. Today, of all these visitors only the typhoons still come.

TYPHOON NOTICE

颶 風 警 號

RED FLAG

FERRIES MAY
STOP RUNNING
AT ANY MOMENT

BLUE FLAG

FERRIES
STOPPED
RUNNING

And of course tourists by the thousands.

They find in Hong Kong excellent service,

endless subjects for photography,

and for the rest, see pages 14–60.

Cheongsam is a Chinese
traditional dress.

In Hong Kong the most modern western techniques
mingle with ancient Chinese ways of doing things.

The heart of Victoria. Big City Hall, big hotels. In the big banks, electronic brains count the profits of big business at lightning speed.

In shops, Chinese brains — plus abacus —
count the profits almost as fast.

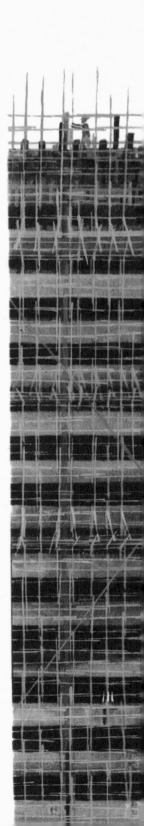

Pedder Street

From behind traditional bamboo scaffolding —

new reinforced concrete buildings continually emerge —

and on traditional bamboo poles, at apartment windows, reinforced Terylene, cotton, and silk do the same.

Silks and brocades —

dried fish —

Without bamboo, hawkers and laborers could not carry
on their businesses, nor carry them around.*

hot chestnuts.

This is not bamboo. It is
sugar cane, eaten like candy.

20

Kai Tak Airport, with a runway built out into Kowloon Bay.*

Jet speed —

tram speed —

Des Voeux Road West

man speed —

There are 818 rickshaws
in Hong Kong.*

woman speed.

There are 57,000 new babies
born in Hong Kong each year.

Don't speed!

A red label under his number
means an English-speaking
policeman.

Pottinger Street

In Hong Kong today live about 6,900,000 people,
ninety-five percent of them Chinese. They speak
mainly Cantonese.

They read nineteen morning papers and ten evening
papers. There are also three English-language dailies.*

Into Hong Kong, short of space and short of water, have come many thousands of refugees from mainland China, seeking jobs and security.

The majority started as squatters on hillsides above town, or even on rooftops in town.

The Hong Kong government carries on the world's largest resettlement scheme. It has already provided homes for more than half a million people in resettlement estates. Monthly rents here average $2.50 (U.S.).*

Thousands of Hong Kong's inhabitants live on boats, the "water people."
They comprise the Tanka and Hoklo ethnic groups. Reportedly some of
them have never set foot on dry land.

The Hong Kong fishing fleet is the largest in Asia: 4,630 vessels,
most of them ocean-going.

There are small and large junks, often diesel-powered —
and sampans, for carrying passengers and small loads, or
just used as homes, complete with chicken yard.

Many sea dwellers are brought ashore to be dried —

many land dwellers go afloat to be fed.

A floating restaurant below Castle Peak.

Aberdeen is among the biggest of the water people's communities, population 6,000. For the boat people, there are floating shops, schools, and even water-borne clinics.* For the tourists at Aberdeen there are two renowned floating restaurants.

Hong Kong's cooking is world famous, and its menus are worldwide — European, American, and every sort of Far Eastern.

Chinese cooking could not exist without rice,

nor Chinese eating without chopsticks.

One famous Chinese delicacy is Peking duck. Its honey coating is sometimes glazed right in the street.

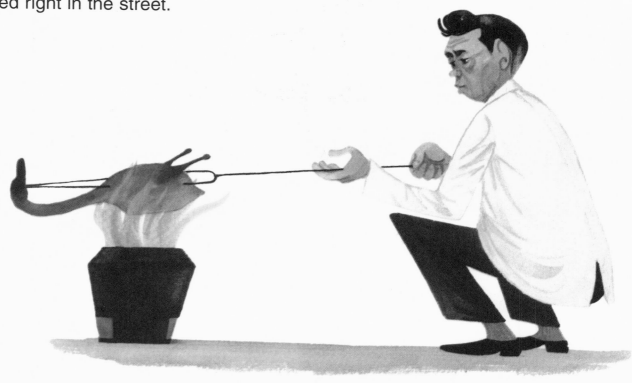

A simple street-restaurant, typical of hundreds.

The umbrellas protect the freshness and greenness of these vegetables from the sun. The Chinese way of cooking brings them to the table almost as fresh and green.

This amah is buying mangoes for dessert. "Amah" is Chinese for domestic helper.

Another Chinese delicacy is preserved duck eggs. They are not a thousand years old; they taste and smell good. This man has them in that basket at the very front.

Everything in this food shop is dried. Small and large fish, egg yolks, squabs, and the sausages on their bright green and violet strings. In the red shrine three joss sticks are burning to bring prosperity to the shop.

Three great and ancient Oriental religions have influenced the Chinese: Buddhism, Confucianism, and Taoism. Ten percent of the population is Christian.

The Temple of Ten Thousand Buddhas at Sha Tin in the New Territories.

Most Chinese families have a picture of the Kitchen God. A week before the Chinese New Year he goes for "home leave" to heaven and there reports to the Jade Emperor on the doings of the household. He returns just in time for the New Year's celebration — the most important of all Chinese festivals.

KUNG HEI FAT CHOY! A PROSPEROUS NEW YEAR!
Firecrackers, festoons, firecrackers, festivities, firecrackers, bangs to
frighten off evil spirits —

Flowers —

peach blossoms for good luck —

'lucky money' for children —

new clothes for everybody —

and a rare chance for a few days off.

On such days the Hong Kong people can join the tourists
who flock to Tiger Balm Garden.

Its white pagoda can be seen from far away.
This is the view from Victoria Park.

It is a sort of Oriental Disneyland whose statues symbolize stories from Chinese mythology and history.* It was built and given to the people of Hong Kong by a Chinese philanthropist. It is named after the patent medicine on which its donor's fortune was based.

There were times when it was quite easy, in order to see all this, to get on a train at Victoria Station in London, and after a two-week journey across Europe, Russia, and China to Canton and Lowu, to arrive at Kowloon, for example with this train at 5:28 P.M.

Lowu on the Shum Chun River is the last Hong Kong stop on the Kowloon–Canton Railway. The bridge marks the crossing point between Hong Kong and mainland China. Sixty million trips are made every year in each direction.

This is one place from which a tourist can peer into China — over rice fields and fish ponds at Lok Ma Chau.* The hills on the horizon are on mainland China.

The New Territories are not blessed with good earth. But the industrious Chinese cultivate every square inch among the ridges and ravines or rotted granite.*

The farmers of the New Territories belong to two groups:

the Cantonese —

and the Hakka.

You can tell them apart by their hats.*

A water buffalo — the tractor of the New Territories.

Good luck scrolls at the door of a village house.

A few steps off the road — graves of rich and poor. The earthenware jars contain the bones. At the Ching Ming Festival, families travel to visit the tombs of their ancestors.

A view of Tolo Harbour, New Territories.

At Tai Po, along the shore, in an ultramodern factory visitors can see an ancient Chinese art — carpet-making.

One of the most ancient of Chinese arts is that of writing.

Written Chinese is a picture language. Every word has its own character or combination of characters. There are thousands of Chinese ideographs.

No wonder these school children look preoccupied.

Queen's Road East

The difficulty of the written language generates business for public scribes.

In the open, a one-man Signboard Carving Factory.

The hand-carved sign over his store says — from right to left —
THE VIRTUE AND LONG-LIFE COFFIN SHOP.

More tempting for the tourists is the sign over this store. Here they can get platinum, gold, silver, diamonds, pearls, sapphires, rubies, emeralds, and the Stone of Heaven — jade — at low prices. Anyone tempted to acquire his jewelry at no price at all may instead take delivery of a load of buckshot.*

The guard of another shop nearby uses a more sporting weapon.

54

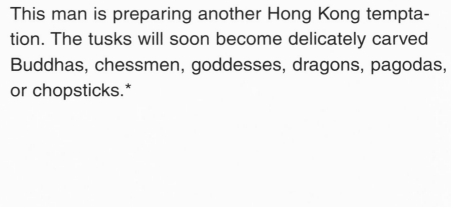

This man is preparing another Hong Kong temptation. The tusks will soon become delicately carved Buddhas, chessmen, goddesses, dragons, pagodas, or chopsticks.*

To shoppers Hong Kong
spells temptation.

56

You can get every kind of goods, local or foreign. It is a free port; prices are very low, on imported goods lower than in their country of origin. Silks, brocades, woolens — tailored to measure in twenty-four hours — embroideries, cameras, binoculars, electronics, watches, crocodile shoes and bags, furs, cars, boats, Arabian camel saddles, everything the greediest shopper may desire.

In short, you can ruin yourself — but think of the money you'll save!

This is Hong Kong. Guidebooks call it "The Pearl of the Far East"; the Chinese call it 香港, which means "Fragrant Harbour." No phrase can convey the astounding beauty of its scenery, or the vitality and the winning charm of its people.

That which enters the eye will never leave the heart.
(A Chinese proverb.)

THIS IS HONG KONG . . . TODAY!

*Page 6: Today Hong Kong is a Special Administrative Region of the People's Republic of China. Victoria is divided into three districts and, lacking formal administrative status, cannot really be considered a true city. It is also not the capital, though many government and administrative offices are located there and it is the central trade and financial district of Hong Kong. Nowadays it is rarely called Victoria City.

*Page 19: Today bamboo is used primarily for scaffolding.

*Page 21: Today Kai Tak Airport no longer exists. It closed on July 6, 1998, and the new Hong Kong International Airport (locally known as Chek Lap Kok Airport) opened on the same day off Lantau Island.

*Page 22: Today there are far fewer rickshaws and they are used mainly for fun rides and photo sessions.

*Page 24: Today you can read forty-nine daily newspapers: twenty-three are Chinese language, thirteen are English (including one in Braille), plus eight bilingual dailies and five in other languages.

*Page 25: Today the Hong Kong government no longer operates a resettlement scheme; the majority of refugees fled China during the post-war period.

*Page 29: Today there are no longer floating schools, shops, or clinics.

*Page 40: Today Hong Kong has a real Disneyland, which opened on Lantau Island in 2005.

*Page 43: Today Lok Ma Chau is a highly trafficked entry point for trucks crossing between Hong Kong and the mainland.

*Page 44: Today sixty percent of the New Territories is country park; the rest has been transformed into a densely-populated area teeming with commercial activity and residential high-rises.

*Page 45: Today only the Hakka have retained their distinctive hats.

*Page 54: Today stores use video surveillance to secure their merchandise. Hong Kong has strict firearms controls, which makes it very difficult to own a gun.

*Page 55: Today international trade in ivory elephant tusks is banned to protect the endangered species.

AND

Today Hong Kong has added a host of attractions, including the Giant Buddha, standing 111 feet tall and weighing 220 tons; Ocean Park, where you can view 250 species of fish, gaze on the South China Sea from a cable car, wander through a butterfly house, and feed panda bears; the Bank of China Tower, a stunning landmark designed by renowned architect I.M. Pei; the Hong Kong Heritage Museum, a rich repository of the culture and arts of early Hong Kong; and A Symphony of Lights, a spectacular multimedia show synchronized to music and narration.